The Ultimate

Fondue
Cookbook

1200 Days of Delicious & Creamy Recipes for Any Occasion

Jen Russell

Table of Contents

INTRODUCTION

Originally, fondue was introduced as a creative way to use up old cheese ends and stale bread to prevent waste. Melted cheese is served in a communal pot as fondue. It is placed on a portable stove that is powered by a candle or a spirit lamp. It is typically served with bread, blanched vegetables, or even fruits.

Fondue's transformation from a Swiss specialty to an international favorite began in Europe's ski resorts in the late 1950s. The Swiss, however, were not the only ones to discover the joys of cooking food communally in a large pot. Hot pot parties are popular ways for Asians to celebrate Chinese New Year, China's largest traditional holiday. Everyone gathers around the hot pot, which is traditionally a large copper pot with a chimney in the center, and cooks a variety of meats, seafood, and vegetables in a simmering broth. At the end of the meal, the hostess ladles out the broth, which has become richly flavored as a result of all the dipped foods.

The 1960s were when fondue first gained popularity in the US. People in North America are still most familiar with the melting types of fondue. Fondue's popularity peaked in the 1960s and 1970s, when it became a house party staple. Cheese fondue was joined in the late 1960s by chocolate dessert fondues, which were made by melting rich chocolate with cream and serving it with fresh fruit or cake for dipping.

Fondues with melted cheese and chocolate continue to be popular. The types of cheese used include French Brie or Italian Parmigiano-Reggiano as well as Swiss Gruyère and Emmental. Similarly, chocolate fondues have come a long way since the mid-1960s, when a chef at New York's Chalet Swiss restaurant served a bar of Toblerone chocolate melted with cream and strawberries for dipping to journalists.

Fondue is not only delicious, but it also has endless possibilities, such as using different cheeses, seasonings, and a wide range of things to dip in it. Fondues can be served as an entrée, a dessert, or a warm or cold appetizer. Soups, casseroles, stews, and even punch can be transformed into fondues with a little imagination. A fondue night is ideal for a casual, interactive, and enjoyable dining experience. Sitting around the fondue pot with your loved ones is possibly the best way to spend an evening together. It allows you to enjoy each other's company while sharing delicious food.

This cookbook can teach you how to prepare fondue. The Fondue Cookbook will reveal insider tips on how to make your own delicious and inviting fondue. You will discover how to prepare numerous cheese fondues, spreads, dips, and sauces.

The cookbook contains over 50 quick and easy recipes with simple instructions. Additionally, it offers a selection of savory and sweet fondue recipes to satisfy everyone's preferences. The cookbook will assist you in creating memorable meals. Your family and friends will keep returning for more because to the recipes' delicious flavors. This book's ingredients are straightforward and readily available at your neighborhood grocery shop. A wonderful fondue may be made with a little planning and a few ingredients. If you use these recipes in a contest, you will undoubtedly win. This book contains the best fondue recipes, ranging from the traditional Swiss cheese fondue to the Mexican queso recipe. All you have to do is buy high-quality ingredients and follow the simple recipes! If you are ready to step into the world of delicious, and perfectly melted fondues, then let us get started.

CHAPTER 1: FONDUE FUNDAMENTALS

What is Fondue?

Fondue, in its most basic form, is a sweet or savory hot dish served in a communal pot with long-handled forks and a variety of accompanying dips and sauces. Fondre is a French word that means "to melt," and cheese fondue was first documented in France in the early 1700s as nothing more than warmed wine mixed with melted cheese and served with bread for dipping. In the early 1900s, the addition of cornstarch modernized fondue in Switzerland, resulting in the smooth, emulsified cheese fondue we know today.

There is another type of fondue found throughout Asia that uses a bubbling pot of richly flavored broth to cook meats, seafood, and vegetables. In China it is called hot pot, and in Japan it is called shabu shabu. It is paired with a bowl of noodles or steamed rice to mop up the delectable broth. Fondue can be a filling meal, so cooking with broth provides a lighter option without sacrificing flavor.

Switzerland has more to offer than just exceptional cheese; it also has some of the best chocolate in the world. It was only a matter of time before high-quality chocolate was melted and served as a dessert fondue, accompanied by fresh fruit and cubes of cake and pastries.

No matter the style of fondue you choose to prepare, one thing remains the same: the company. Fondue is a timeless experience for you and your guests to enjoy together, sharing an atmosphere of coziness and warmth around the table.

Techniques in Making Fondue

Cheese Fondues

To add flavor, rub the cut side of a garlic clove into the fondue pot. To help cheese melt quickly, grate or crumble it, and heat it gently because it burns easily.

Oil Fondues

Use a kitchen thermometer to check the oil's temperature. 190°C/375°F should be the setting. Once the oil has been transferred to the pot, turn the heat up to its highest position.

When oil is overheated, it degrades and becomes a greasy, frothy mass.

Wine and Herb Fondues

Pour wine or flavoring liquid into the pot, add the cheese and set over the flame. Grate or crumble the cheese and cover it with a tight-fitting lid to prevent scorching and evaporating too much liquid.

When the cheese has melted, add more wine until it bubbles as it cooks. Until the appropriate consistency is attained, cook over low heat.

Don't let fondue pots overheat - they will burn the oil in them and become useless. Above all, never leave a pot unattended when it is over the flame.

A word about the wine you use for fondues: The ingredients of the cheese fondue dictate the wine to use. The wine choice for hard cheeses like Gruyère or Emmentaler is a dry white wine such as a dry Riesling An off-dry wine like Pinot Gris, Spatlese or Gewürztraminer is perfect for medium cheeses (Emmental or young Alpine cheeses). For soft cheeses like Raclette or Brunost, you should choose a sweet wine like a German Riesling or a late-harvest wine.

Tips and Tricks to Fondue

Fondue recipes vary greatly. You have an infinite number of fondue pot recipes and dipping ingredients to prepare. You can even vary the sauce accompaniments as needed. You practically have an advantage in making everyone's fondue experience memorable and gastronomically pleasurable.

Take a cue from the following tips to help you make everything perfect:

The crust that forms at the bottom of a cheese fondue should never be removed. It is known as "la religieuse" or "la croute" Switzerland. After being scraped from the pan, it is offered to visitors as a delicacy.

Before serving, trim and slice the meat. You could even marinate it. It is best to precook meats before dipping them in a low-temperature fondue, such as cheese fondue.

To retain the color of your prepared fruits and vegetables, give them a good squeeze of lemon juice.

Prepare raw meats in separate trays to avoid contamination of the other ingredients. Before using it, keep the meat refrigerated in the refrigerator.

Pat dry meat and vegetables to prevent dangerous spatters when dipped into hot fondue.

Meat broths must match the meat - beef on beef broth, chicken on chicken broth.

Keep an eye on your fondue pot, especially if it's extremely hot and there are children nearby.

The amount of time you must keep your food ingredient dipped in fondue depends on the type of food and the temperature in which it is dipped.

Never use freshly baked bread or cakes. They have to be at least one day old. Slices of bread and cakes that are one day old are firm and will not crumble when dipped in fondue.

Keep the fruits cold before dipping to make sure the sauce sticks to them.

A fondue pot should be shared by no more than four people.

When hosting a fondue party, decide which course you will assign the fondue to. Never serve it as an appetizer, main course, and dessert all at the same time.

Fill the fondue pot only halfway. This is done to prevent spattering when people begin to dip their food.

To determine how much food to prepare for your guests, the rule of thumb is half a pound of food for each person, assuming you are also serving other entrées.

Refrigerate any leftover fondue in an airtight container. It can last 1 to 2 days. Additionally, it can be prepared in advance and kept in the refrigerator.

Place the desired amount of fondue in a double boiler and heat to the desired temperature.

Add a little wine if the fondue gets too thick.

Make sure not to overcook the fondue unless otherwise specified, as the cheese tends to become stringy.

Serve fondue with bite-size dippers like boiled new potatoes, lightly steamed vegetables like broccoli, asparagus and cauliflower, mushrooms, tomatoes, bread, fruits like apple and pear, crackers, carrots, cucumber, bell peppers, pretzels, breadsticks, pickled vegetables, sausages, potato chips, tortilla chips, pita chips, ham, chicken pieces, grilled steak etc.

Do's and Don'ts of Fondue

While you don't need to have a party to have some fondue, eating fondue remains a communal experience. Also, no matter how exclusive your guest list is or how pricey your ingredients are, a fondue meal has a casual air. Despite this, there are a few rules to ensure everybody's safety and comfort:

Never fill a pot with oil fondue more than 13 percent full. If the fondue pot needs to be reheated or requires more oil, move it away from the heat source and away from your guests. Refresh the oil in the kitchen, then return the pot to the table with care.

Never refuel an alcoholic pot while it is still warm. Before adding fuel, the burner attachment must be completely cool.

Always pay close attention to the directions that come with your fondue set. The requirements and procedures for various heat sources differ slightly.

Make sure you have enough plates, skewers, forks, and dipping bowls to prevent your guests from re-dipping previously nibbled items into the fondue pot or sauce bowls.

Bread, veggies, and other ready-to-eat meals should be stored apart from raw meats and shellfish. Meats and seafood that have been prepared should either be served right away or covered and chilled until ready to serve.

Prepare antibacterial wipes to clean up spills or dropped ingredients.

Salmonella can be found in raw eggs. Some Asian hot pots include a raw egg dipping sauce. Consider using pasteurized eggs or avoid raw egg sauces altogether.

Oil and broth fondue mixtures must remain hot enough to thoroughly cook meats and shellfish.

Finally, to avoid the problem of double-dipping, put a large basket of skewers next to the fondue pot. Put regular forks at everyone's place, or a basket of regular or disposable forks next to buffet plates. Your guests will quickly get the idea—dunk with the skewers, move the food onto a plate, and eat with a regular fork. In the case of vegetables, fruits, or long chunks of bread, guests can just dip one end into the pot. Remember these simple health and safety tips, and have fun fondue-ing!

CHAPTER 2: TOOLS AND EQUIPMENT

While you can always use any other pot, having the proper equipment is a must, especially if you are hosting an event and you want it to be memorable for everyone.

Basically, there's a pot, a heating source, and a couple of sticks or forks. The pot is where the fondue goes, kept warm by gentle heat. The forks, on the other hand, are for the diners. So, they would have something to thread the food bits into before dipping or dunking them into the fondue. Some fondue sets even come with plates and Lazy Susans to make serving fun.

There are varying fondue sets available in the market. The pots come in different sizes and are made of different materials. The basic equipment for cheese-based fondues is usually made of ceramic and is heated with a gel-based or alcohol-based fuel. You can use similar equipment (fondue fountain) for your sweet fondues like the classic chocolate but usually, they are of a smaller size.

Different Types of Fondue Makers

Because there are so many various types of fondue available on the market today, all with distinct materials and styles, choose the best brand can be challenging. You may choose the type of fondue maker you want to buy by looking at the options we have gathered.

Enameled Cast Iron

Enameled cast iron, like regular cast iron, distributes heat evenly across the entire pot, preventing hot and cold spots in the cheese while also minimizing stirring.

Ceramic Fondue Set

Ceramic fondue pots are proven to be long-lasting, sturdy, and easy to clean. When cooking classic Swiss cheese fondues, a porcelain fondue pot is typically used.

Electric Fondue Pots

There is an electric Fondue pot as well as a typical cheese fondue that employs a flame as a heat source.

Fondue Fountain

As you may have noticed, the majority of the fondue pots described above are built around a pot and a heat source. The Fondue Fountain is another Fondue variant available here.

Desserts are often served from a fondue fountain, with chocolate fondue being the most popular. This running fountain maintains the temperature of melted chocolate (similar to that of a fountain). The idea behind this method is to keep the fondue at a constant temperature while keeping the chocolate liquid.

Fondue fountains could look attractive when arranged at a table; the only issue is the cleaning process. Cleaning the fondue fountain might be challenging; some individuals choose to disassemble the apparatus to clean it completely. You can hand wash the parts after taking them apart.

Combination Fondue Burner

The Fondue burner allows customers to modify the temperature control of the machine to regulate the temperature based on how much cheese they want to melt and how well they want their meat to be cooked.

It has a nonstick coating, so food residue, like melted cheese, will not stick to its surface, making it easy to clean.

Boska Holland Tealight Fondue Set

Boska's Fondue set works with both chocolate and cheese. The saucepan is microwave safe, so you can quickly produce melted cheese and melted chocolate.

Choosing The Right Fondue Pot

This section provides a detailed guide on how to select the appropriate type of fondue pot that's suited to the cooking requirements of the fondue you have chosen to prepare. Nothing is more frustrating than putting in all the effort to prepare a fondue feast only to scorch it or, worse, end up with a cracked fondue pot that can't withstand the higher heat of hot oil or broth-style fondue. The following list will assist you in selecting a pot as well as provide tips on how to confidently host a successful fondue party from start to finish. If you already have a fondue pot, read the manufacturer's instructions to understand what it can and cannot do.

Enameled Cast-Iron Fondue Pots

This style of fondue pot comes with an open-flame style burner that sits underneath the pot and requires liquid Sterno or another ethanol-based gel fuel to burn. These pots go from stove to table, and the small burners aren't strong enough to properly heat oil or broth-based fondue for very long. They can be an option for dessert fondue, although the pot is typically too large for the smaller serving size of this fondue variety. Aesthetically, this style of fondue pot will look the part on your table, adding to the cozy atmosphere of a traditional Swiss cheese fondue party.

Stainless Steel and Aluminum Fondue Pots

Hot oil and broth-style fondues, such as fondue Bourguignonne and Hot Pot, are best served in stainless steel or aluminum fondue pots. They are thin and lightweight, and they heat up quickly, ensuring that your meat and vegetables are thoroughly cooked. Unless they come with a ceramic insert, these pots are not recommended for cheese and dessert fondue. The stainless steel and aluminum pot's thin bottom will quickly scorch the cheese and dessert fondue, making your meal difficult to enjoy and a big mess to clean up. This type of fondue pot frequently comes with a splash guard that sits on top of the pot and helps prevent hot oil and broth splatters on your table and your guests.

Glazed Ceramic Fondue Pots

Glazed ceramic fondue pots come in a variety of sizes and are suitable for both cheese and dessert fondue. Larger ceramic vessels frequently include an open-flame burner, similar to an enameled cast-iron pot, whereas smaller sets typically include a tealight candle as the heat source, which produces significantly less heat. As a result, the latter is ideal for keeping dessert fondue warm without becoming too hot. Glazed ceramic will crack or break if subjected to the high heat required for hot oil and broth-style fondue. Consider a smaller glazed ceramic fondue pot if you only intend to serve cheese or dessert fondue and have limited space.

CHAPTER 3: 50 RECIPES

1. Classic Cheese Fondue

Prep time: 10 mins

Cooking time: 40 mins

Servings: 12

Ingredients:

- 300g Alpine-style cheese, grated
- 300g gouda cheese, grated
- 300g fontina cheese, grated
- 4 tbsp cornstarch
- 2 cloves garlic, peeled, minced
- 2 tbsp brandy
- 1/4 tsp ground nutmeg
- 2 c. dry white wine
- 2 tbsp freshly squeezed lemon juice
- 2 tsp Dijon mustard

Directions:

1. Add all the varieties of cheese into a bowl. Sprinkle cornstarch over the cheese and toss well.
2. Place a heatproof fondue pot or heavy saucepan over medium-low heat. Add wine, lemon juice and garlic and stir.
3. When the mixture begins to simmer, add the cheese mixture into the pot, a tbsp at a time and mix well each time.
4. When all of it is added, stir until smooth.
5. Add brandy, nutmeg and mustard and stir well.
6. Turn off the heat. Serve warm.

2. Swiss Cheese Fondue

Prep time: 10 mins

Cooking time: 30 mins

Servings: 4

Ingredients:

- 1 small clove garlic, peeled, halved
- 3 tsp cornstarch
- 1/8 tsp ground nutmeg
- 1/2 c. dry white wine
- 1/2 tsp freshly squeezed lemon juice
- Freshly ground pepper to taste
- 3/4 tbsp kirsch
- 114g Emmental cheese or any other Swiss cheese, grated
- 230g Gruyere cheese, grated

Directions:

1. Cut garlic into 2 halves and rub the inside of the fondue pot with it. Throw away the garlic cloves.

2. Add all the varieties of cheese into the fondue pot. Add lemon juice, cornstarch and wine and whisk thoroughly.

3. Place the pot over medium-low heat. Cook until the cheese begins to melt. Stir occasionally.

4. Stir in kirsch, nutmeg and pepper and stir until smooth. Turn off the heat.

5. Serve hot.

3. Beer Cheese Fondue

Prep time: 10 mins

Cooking time: 20 mins

Servings: 3 – 4

Ingredients:

- 1/2 c. Pilsner-style beer
- 1/2 tbsp cornstarch
- 1/4 tsp Worcestershire sauce
- Fine sea salt to taste
- 230g gruyere cheese, shredded
- 1 tsp Sweet Bavarian mustard or Dijon mustard
- 1/8 tsp paprika or to taste

Directions:

1. Pour beer into a fondue pot or heavy saucepan. Place the pot over medium-high heat.
2. When it begins to boil, lower the heat and let it simmer.
3. Sprinkle cornstarch over the cheese and toss well.
4. Add the cheese mixture into the pot, a tbsp at a time and mix well each time.
5. When all of it is added, stir until smooth.
6. Add Worcestershire sauce, mustard, salt and paprika and mix well. Turn off the heat.
7. Serve hot.

4.   Smoked Mozzarella Fondue

Prep time: 10 min

Cooking time: 30

Servings: 3 – 4

Ingredients:

- 115g cream cheese, at room temperature
- 1/2 c. grated provolone cheese
- 1/2c. smoked mozzarella cheese
- 1/4 c. freshly grated parmesan cheese
- 1/4 tsp dried thyme
- 1/8 tsp red pepper flakes
- Freshly ground pepper to taste
- 1/4 tsp Italian seasoning
- Salt to taste
- 1/2 Tbsp finely chopped parsley
- 3 Tbsp sour cream
- 1/2 small tomato, chopped

Directions:

1. Add cream cheese, sour cream, seasonings, salt, thyme and all the cheeses into a baking dish and mix until well combined.

2. Bake in a preheated oven at 350° F for 20 mins.

3. Set the oven to broil mode and broil for a few minutes until brown on top.

4. Top with tomato and parsley and serve.

5. Porcini Fondue

Prep time: 10 mins

Cooking time: 40 mins

Servings: 3

Ingredients:

- 15g dried porcini mushrooms
- 1/2 c. hot water
- 2 small cloves garlic, peeled, minced
- 1 tsp cornstarch
- 1 c. grated, packed Emmental cheese
- 1 c. grated, packed Gruyere cheese
- 10 tbsp Sauvignon Blank or any other dry white wine of your choice
- Salt to taste
- Pepper to taste

Directions:

1. Place porcini mushrooms in a bowl. Pour hot water over it. Let it rehydrate for about 30 mins.
2. Take out the mushrooms from the soaked water and place them on your cutting board. Chop into fine pieces. Do not discard the soaked water.
3. Pour the soaked water into a skillet, but do not add the particles that are at the bottom of the bowl.
4. Add mushrooms to the soaked water in the skillet along with garlic. Place the skillet over medium heat and cook until nearly dry. Add salt and pepper to taste. Turn off the heat.
5. Meanwhile, add all the cheeses into a bowl and toss well.
6. Add 1/2 tbsp wine and cornstarch into a bowl and stir well.
7. Pour the remaining wine into a saucepan. Place the saucepan over medium-high heat.
8. Add the cheese mixture into the pot, 3 to 4 tbsp at a time and mix well each time.
9. When all of it is added, stir until smooth. Stir in the cornstarch mixture.
10. Stir constantly until slightly thick. Let it simmer for a couple of minutes. Taste and adjust the seasonings if required. Turn off the heat.
11. Transfer into a serving bowl. Add porcini and stir
12. Serve hot or warm. It tastes great with ham and Ciabatta.

6. Greek Fondue

Prep time: 10 mins

Cooking time: 30 mins

Servings: 4

Ingredients:

- 1/2 tbsp olive oil
- 115g cream cheese, softened
- 1/2 c. shredded mozzarella cheese
- 1/2 c. crumbled feta cheese
- 2 tbsp whole milk
- 3 tbsp Greek yogurt
- 1 tbsp lemon juice
- 1/2 tsp grated lemon zest
- Kosher salt to taste
- 1/8 tsp red pepper flakes
- Freshly ground pepper to taste
- 1/2 tbsp chopped parsley
- 1/2 tbsp chopped dill

To garnish:

- 1/2tbsp chopped parsley
- 1/2 tbsp chopped dill
- 1/4/c. sliced kalamata olives
- 1/2 c. halved cherry tomatoes
- Olive oil, as required

Directions:

1. Place a skillet over medium heat. Add oil
2. When the oil is heated, add garlic and sauté for a few seconds until aromatic.
3. Stir in the cream cheese. Break it simultaneously as it melts.
4. Add milk and whisk well. Heat thoroughly.

5. Add the rest of the ingredients and mix well. Heat until the cheese melts completely and the mixture is smooth. Stir occasionally. Turn off the heat.

6. Transfer into a serving bowl. Drizzle oil on top. Sprinkle dill, parsley, tomatoes and olives and serve.

7. Caramelized Shallot and Gruyere Cheese Fondue

Prep time: 10 mins

Cooking time: 25 mins

Servings: 4

Ingredients:

- 1/2 tbsp butter
- 1/2 tsp sugar
- 1 ¾ c. packed, finely grated gruyere cheese
- 3/4c. dry white wine or more if required
- 2 small cloves garlic, finely grated
- Freshly ground pepper to taste
- 3/4c. thinly sliced shallots
- 1/2tsp salt or to taste
- 1 tbsp all-purpose flour or cornstarch
- 1/8 tsp ground nutmeg
- 1 tbsp apple brandy

Directions:

1. Place cheese in a bowl. Sprinkle flour over it and toss well.
2. Place a heavy-bottomed saucepan or fondue pot over medium heat. Add butter. When butter melts, add shallots and sauté for a couple of minutes.
3. Stir in the sugar and salt and cook for 8 – 10 mins.
4. Stir in the wine.
5. When it begins to simmer, add the cheese mixture into the pot, 2 to 3 heaping tbsp at a time and mix well each time.
6. When all of it is added, stir until smooth. Add more wine if you want to dilute the fondue.
7. Add brandy, garlic, nutmeg, salt and a generous amount of pepper and stir. Turn off the heat. Pour into a bowl.
8. Serve hot.

8. French Onion Fondue

Prep time: 10 mins

Cooking time: 20 mins

Servings: 8

Ingredients:

- 6 tbsp butter

- 1 c. dry white wine

- Freshly ground pepper to taste

- 3 c. finely chopped onion

- 24 slices Deli American cheese, chopped

Directions:

1. Place a heavy saucepan or fondue pot over medium heat. Add butter. When butter melts, add onions and sauté until golden brown in color.

2. Stir in wine. When it begins to simmer, add the cheese mixture into the pot, a handful at a time and mix well each time.

3. When all of it is added, stir until smooth. Add pepper to taste.

9. Sour Cream Fondue

Prep time: 10 mins

Cooking time: 10 mins

Servings: 3

Ingredients

- 2 c. canned pineapple chunks
- 3 tbsp liquid honey
- 3 tbsp pineapple juice (reserved from the can)
- 1½ c. sour cream

Directions.

1. Dry the pineapple chunks.
2. Combine the sour cream, honey, and pineapple juice.
3. Chill briefly until the fondue starts to set. Use dipping forks to dip the pineapple chunks into the sour cream.

10. Chocolate Zucchini Fondue

Prep time: 10 mins

Cooking time: 20 mins

Servings: 3

Ingredients

- 4 zucchini
- 1 tsp almond extract
- 1¾ c. chocolate chips
- 1 tbsp plus 1 tsp instant hot chocolate
- 1/2 c. plus 2 tbsp evaporated milk
- 1/2 tsp cinnamon
- 2 tsp vanilla extract
- 1 tbsp kirsch

Directions

1. Wash the zucchini, peel, and cut diagonally into slices approximately 1/4 - 1/2 inch thick. Cut in half again.

2. Combine the chocolate chips, evaporated milk, vanilla extract, and almond extract in a metal bowl and place on top of a saucepan half-filled with simmering water. Melt the chocolate on low to medium-low heat, stirring frequently and making sure that it doesn't boil. Stir in the cocoa, cinnamon, and kirsch.

3. Transfer the fondue mixture to the fondue pot and set it on the burner. Keep the fondue warm on low heat. Serve with the zucchini slices for dipping.

11. Mini-Waffle Fondue

Prep time: 10 mins

Cooking time: 30 mins

Servings: 3

Ingredients:

- 12 mini-waffles, mini-pancakes or fingers of French toast
- 1 pinch ground cinnamon
- 1/4 tsp. of vanilla extract, pure
- 2 tbsp. of cream cheese, light whipped
- 1/3 c. of syrup, maple or your favorite syrup
- 1 x 15 oz. can of peaches, sliced – you can use juice too.

Directions:

1. Combine the cinnamon, vanilla, cream cheese, syrup and peaches in a food processor. Purée until the mixture is smooth. There can be some cheese lumps showing at this time. They'll be gone in step 2.

2. Pour mixture into the pot. Warm on med-high and stir often until the cream cheese has melted and the sauce bubbles around the edges.

3. Serve in a large bowl with mini-waffles or mini pancakes.

4. Use fingers for dipping, but don't double-dip.

12. Cinnamon Roll Breakfast Fondue

Prep **time**: 10 mins

Cooking time: 20 mins

Servings: 3

Ingredients:

- 1 x 6 oz. carton of Greek yogurt, honey vanilla
- 1/2 c. of crushed cereal of choice
- 1 c. of strawberries
- 2 sliced bananas
- 1 sliced green apple
- 1 tube of cinnamon rolls and icing

Directions:

1. Preheat the oven to 400F.

2. Cover a medium baking sheet using parchment paper.

3. Open cinnamon rolls. Slice all into four round pieces. Bake in the oven for 10 to 14 minutes. They should start to turn brown.

4. Set your table with small bowls of fruit, cinnamon roll cubes, cereal and yogurt.

5. Serve with fondue skewers. Mixing and dipping is a fun breakfast, especially on the weekend, when you won't have to hurry.

13. Cheeseburger Fondue

Prep **time:** 10 mins

Cooking time: 30 mins

Servings: 3

Ingredients:

- 1/4 c. of diced tomatoes, fire-roasted
- 1/4 c. of lettuce, shredded
- 1/4 c. of relish, pickle
- 30 frozen meatballs – cook using directions on the package
- 1 c. of cheddar cheese, grated
- 3/4 c. of beer, light
- 1/4 tsp. of Worcestershire sauce
- 2 tbsp. of flour, all-purpose
- 1/4 tsp. of mustard (ground)
- 2 tbsp. of butter, softened

Directions:

1. Add butter to a saucepan on medium heat. Allow it to melt. Whisk in flour. Cook for a minute.

2. Add beer, Worcestershire sauce and mustard. Whisk continuously until the mixture thickens, in two minutes or so.

3. Remove from the burner. Stir in cheddar cheese. Continue to stir until the sauce is creamy and smooth. Place in a fondue pot or slow cooker to keep it warm.

4. Serve meatballs with toothpicks or fondue forks. Dip meatballs in cheese, then diced tomatoes, lettuce and pickle relish.

14. Tomato & Olive Oil Fondue

Prep time: 10 mins

Cooking time: 20 mins

Servings: 3

Ingredients:

- 4 tbsp. of oil, olive
- 2 pints of tomatoes, cherry
- 1/2 tsp. of salt, kosher
- 1/4 c. of butter, unsalted
- Crusty bread, sliced

Directions:

1. Combine the oil and tomatoes in a skillet on high heat. Stir often while cooking until the tomatoes start to burst. This usually takes about five or six minutes.

2. Reduce the heat to medium-high. Cook and stir often until most tomatoes have broken down, or five to seven minutes.

3. Stir in the salt and butter until the butter melts.

4. Remove from the oven burner. Pour mixture into fondue pot. Serve while hot, with crusty bread.

15. White Wine & Blue Cheese Fondue

Prep **time**: 10 mins

Cooking time: 30 mins

Servings: 3

Ingredients:

- 2 tbsp. of crème fraiche
- 2 tbsp. + 2 tsp. of cornstarch
- 12 oz. of crumbled cheese, British Stilton
- 1 c. of Sauternes
- 1 garlic clove
- Sea salt & pepper, ground

For serving: cubed bread, pickled veggies, beef tips and fingerling potatoes

Directions:

1. Rub inside the fondue pot vigorously with garlic. Discard garlic. Add Sauternes. Bring to a boil on medium heat.

2. In a small bowl, stir cornstarch and Stilton cheese and combine. Once Sauternes comes to a boil, add the cheese mixture slowly and whisk well. Make sure that every addition has been melted and combined before you add more.

3. Once it has cooked for another minute. Whisk in the crème Fraiche, then season using salt & pepper.

4. Remove heat from the pot. Serve with bread and other dippable ingredients of your choice.

16. Chicken & Beef Fondue

Prep time: 10 mins

Cooking time: 30 mins

Servings: 3

Ingredients:

For cucumber sauce

- 1/2 tsp. of sea salt
- 2 tbsp. of onion, chopped
- 1 c. of cucumber, peeled and chopped
- 1/4 c. of milk, whole
- 2 c. of sour cream
- 2 pkg. of softened cream cheese

For fondue sauce

- 4 tsp. of parsley flakes
- 4 peeled garlic cloves
- 2 x 14 oz cans of broth, beef
- 4 x 14 oz cans of broth, chicken
- 2 c. of broccoli florets, fresh, small
- 2 sliced carrots, medium
- 2 cubed bell peppers, your favorite color
- 1 x 8-ounce pkg. of mushrooms, fresh, whole
- 1 pound of chicken breasts, skinless, boneless
- 1 pound of sirloin steak, beef, boneless
- 2 tsp. of thyme leaves, dried
- 1/3 tsp. of salt, coarse
- 1/3 tsp. of pepper, ground

Other dipping sauces as preferred:

- Teriyaki sauce
- Sweet & sour sauce

- Horseradish sauce
- BBQ sauce

Directions:

1. To create the sauce, beat cream cheese until it's creamy in a medium-sized bowl. Stir in the other sauce ingredients. Cover. Refrigerate for two hours or so, until it chills.

2. Cut the chicken and beef into cubes. Blot them dry using paper towels. Place the lettuce on a platter and arrange the meat on them. Cover and refrigerate until you're ready to serve.

3. Arrange the veggies on another plate. Set it aside.

4. When ready to serve, divide the broth into 2 x 3 qt fondue pots. Add roughly 1/2 of salt, pepper, parsley and garlic in each pot. Heat until the mixture is boiling in both pots.

5. Use fondue forks to spear veggies and meats and dip them in hot broth. Cook them for two to four minutes until the meat cooks. Serve with dipping sauces.

17. Roast Pumpkin with Cheese "Fondue"

Prep time: 10 mins

Cooking time: 2 hours

Servings: 3

Ingredients:

- 2 baguettes (15 inches each), cut into ½ inch thick slices
- 3 c. heavy cream
- 1 tsp grated nutmeg
- 5 c. coarsely grated Emmentaler cheese
- 5 c. coarsely grated Gruyere cheese
- 2 tbsp olive oil
- 2 orange pumpkins (3.2 kg each)
- 2 c. chicken or vegetable broth
- Salt to taste
- Pepper to taste

Directions:

1. Place the baguette slices on a baking sheet, in a single layer.
2. Bake in a preheated oven at 450° F for 7 minutes or until crisp on top.
3. Remove from the oven and let it cool.
4. Cut off a thick, round slice, from the stem side of each pumpkin. Retain the tops.
5. Scoop the seeds and membranes from the inside of the pumpkins as well as from the tops of the pumpkins.
6. Sprinkle salt inside the pumpkin.
7. Add both pieces of cheese into a bowl and toss well.
8. Add broth, cream, nutmeg, pepper and salt into a bowl and whisk well.
9. Place a layer of bread on the bottom of the pumpkins. Do not overlap.
10. Sprinkle a cup of cheese over the bread in each of the pumpkins. Spread 1/2 cup of the cream mixture over the cheese layer in each pumpkin.
11. Repeat steps 9 and 10 a few times until the pumpkin is nearly full.
12. Close the pumpkins with the tops.

13. Place the rack in the lower third position in the oven.

14. Grease 2 baking pans with some oil. Grease the pumpkin with oil on the skin side.

15. Bake in a preheated oven at 350° F for about 1 to 2 hours or until the pumpkin is tender.

16. Scoop the pumpkin along with the layered fondue while serving.

18.   Spinach and Artichoke Fondue

Prep **time**: 10 mins

Cooking time: 20 mins

Servings: 3

Ingredients:

- 1 c. shredded mozzarella cheese
- 1 c. shredded gruyere cheese
- 1/2 c. shredded parmesan cheese
- 2/3 c. white cooking wine
- 2 tsp flour
- 2 tbsp minced garlic
- 2/3 c. chopped, drained artichoke hearts
- 1 ½ c. chopped baby spinach

Directions:

1. Add all the varieties of cheese into a bowl and toss well.
2. Sprinkle flour on top. Toss well.
3. Add wine and garlic into a fondue pot or heavy pot. Place the pot over medium-high heat.
4. When it begins to boil, add spinach and artichoke hearts and mix well.
5. Cook until spinach wilts. Add the cheese mixture into the pot, 2 to 3 heaping tablespoons at a time and mix well each time.
6. Stir constantly until the cheese melts and resembles strings.
7. Serve hot.

19. Pizza Fondue

Prep **time**: 10 mins

Cooking time: 40 mins

Servings: 3

Ingredients:

- 1/2 jar marinara sauce
- 3 tbsp freshly grated parmesan cheese
- 1 c. shredded mozzarella cheese + extra to top
- 1/2 package mini pepperoni
- A large pinch dried oregano

Directions:

1. Add marinara sauce, oregano, both the cheeses and half the pepperoni into the fondue pot or heavy-bottomed saucepan.

2. Place the pot over medium heat. Stir frequently until the mixture melts. Turn off the heat.

3. Garnish with mozzarella and pepperoni slices and serve.

20. German-Style Broth & Steak Fondue

Prep time: 10 mins

Cooking time: 20 mins

Servings: 3

Ingredients

- 4 c. of beef broth, low sodium
- 1 c. of wine, white
- 3 sliced onions, green
- 3 minced garlic cloves

For dipping

- Steak cubes
- Broccoli florets
- Cauliflower florets
- Mushrooms

Directions:

1. Heat broth, wine, garlic and green onions in a pan on med till the mixture boils. Reduce heat to simmer.

2. Slice meat into cubes and vegetables in small florets.

3. Transfer broth fondue to your fondue pot with a heat source under it. Serve and cook steak and veggies by dipping and holding in broth. They take about five minutes per chunk to cook.

21. Chili Queso Fondue

Prep **time**: 10 mins

Cooking time: 30 mins

Servings: 3

Ingredients

- 1 chopped tomato, small
- 1 seeded & chopped chile, serrano
- 2 tbsp. of fresh chopped oregano
- Salt, kosher
- 8 oz. of mild cheddar, grated coarsely
- 8 oz. of Monterey Jack cheese, grated coarsely
- 1 tbsp. of flour, all-purpose
- 1 x 4 oz. link of Italian hot sausage or chorizo – remove the casing
- 1/2 c. of onion, minced
- 1/2 c. of lager, light

For dipping

- Tortilla chips

Directions:

1. Mix the chile, tomatoes and oregano in a small mixing bowl. Season using kosher salt, as desired. Allow this salsa to sit for 1/2 hour

2. Toss cheese and flour together in a medium-sized bowl. Cook the chorizo in a pan on medium heat, breaking it up as it cooks till it starts to render. This should happen within a minute. Add the onions. Continue to cook till the chorizo has cooked through and the onions are translucent and soft.

3. Transfer the chorizo mixture to a small-sized bowl and return the pan to medium heat. Add the lager. Stir occasionally while simmering and scrape up browned bits, if any.

4. Add the cheese mixture 1/4 c. after another while constantly whisking. Make sure the mixture is smooth and blended well before you add more cheese. Stir in the chorizo mixture and combine.

5. Spoon the salsa over chile queso. Serve in a fondue pot or skillet with chips.

22. Spinach and Artichoke Fondue

Prep time: 10 mins

Cooking time: 20 mins

Servings: 4

Ingredients

- **1/2** c. mozzarella cheese
- 1/2 c. parmesan cheese
- 3 tbsp all-purpose flour
- 1/3 c. white wine
- 2 tsp minced garlic
- 1 c. artichoke hearts
- 1/2 c. spinach leaves

Directions:

1. We will start by gathering all the ingredients and donning a cooking apron.

2. After this, take half a c. of grated parmesan cheese and half a c. of mozzarella cheese in a large bowl.

3. Add 3 tbsp of all-purpose flour to it. Mix well.

4. Pour 1/3 cup of white wine into a pot, add minced garlic and bring to a boil.

5. Once it starts to boil, add spinach leaves and artichoke hearts to the pot.

6. Secure the lid and cook for 5 minutes.

7. After 5 minutes, add the grated cheese mixture to it. Cook for a few more minutes.

8. Transfer to a fondue pot and light the candle.

9. You can serve it with bread crumbs.

23. Smoked brisket with cheese Fondue

Prep time: 10 mins

Cooking time: 30 mins

Servings: 4

Ingredients:

For brisket

- 3 slices brisket
- Salt as required
- Black pepper as required
- 2 tsp garlic
- For cheese fondue
- 1 boiled potato
- 1 tsp olive oil
- 2 tsp oregano
- 2 tsp garlic paste
- Salt as required
- 1 tomato
- 1 tbsp butter
- 2 tbsp all-purpose flour
- 1 c. milk
- 3 cheese slices
- 1/2 c. mozzarella cheese

Directions:

1. Season the brisket slices with salt and black pepper.
2. Coat it well with garlic powder and smoke it for thirty to forty minutes until the brisket turns brown.
3. Meanwhile, prepare the cheese fondue. Start by heating oil in a pan. Add a teaspoon of oregano and garlic paste to it.
4. Chop a boiled potato and add it to the pan.
5. Sprinkle some salt. Stir for some time and transfer to a plate.

6. In the same pan, add oregano and garlic paste. Add chopped tomato to it. Sauté well. Once done, transfer to a plate.

7. Heat butter in a pan and add all-purpose flour to it. Keep stirring to prevent lumps from forming.

8. Pour a cup of milk into the pan. Add three cheese slices to it.

9. Follow it with 1/2 cup of mozzarella cheese. Mix well.

10. Transfer the cheese mixture to a fondue pot.

11. Serve with smoked brisket.

Enjoy!

24. Meat fondue

Prep time: 10 mins

Cooking time: 30 mins

Servings: 4

Ingredients:

- 5 oz beef tenderloin
- 1 c. vegetable oil
- 5 oz chicken breast
- Salt as required
- Black pepper as required

Directions:

1. Wash beef as well as chicken breast properly.
2. Chop it into small cubes.
3. Season well with salt and black pepper.
4. Add a teaspoon of vegetable oil to it. Let it marinate.
5. After this, put the remaining c. of oil in the fondue pot.
6. Once it heats up, using a skewer, put a cube of meat in it. Cook until it turns brown.
7. You can do two or three cubes at once.
8. Serve hot with various sauces. Enjoy!

25. Broth fondue

Prep time: 10 mins

Cooking time: 20 mins

Servings: 4

Ingredients:

- 2 c. beef broth
- 2 cloves of garlic
- 3 tbsp water
- 1/5 c. soy sauce
- Salt and black pepper as required

Directions:

1. Heat a fondue pot and light the candle.
2. Take two cups of beef broth in a pot.
3. Add two cloves of garlic and 3 tbsp of water. Mix well
4. Now, put soy sauce in it.
5. Sprinkle some salt and black pepper according to your preference.
6. Lower the flame and dunk the dips in it. As mentioned above, you can use a variety of things as dippers.
7. Enjoy hot.

26. Orange Chocolate Fondue

Prep time: 10 mins

Cooking time: 20 mins

Servings: 4

Ingredients:

- 1/2 c. double cream
- 1 tsp orange liqueur
- 1 tsp vanilla extract
- 1 c. orange chocolate

Directions:

1. Take half a cup of double cream, a teaspoon of orange liqueur, a teaspoon of vanilla extract, and a c. of orange chocolate in a microwave-friendly bowl.

2. Microwave for a few seconds. Transfer to a fondue pot.

3. Serve with strawberries or marshmallows, whatever you like.

27. Pesto Fondue

Prep time: 10 mins

Cooking time: 15 Minutes

Servings: 4

Ingredients:

- 2 tbsp white wine
- 1⅓ c. grated cheese
- Salt as required
- Black pepper as required
- 2 tsp minced garlic
- 1/3 c. hazelnuts
- 1/2 c. basil leaves
- 2 tbsp olive oil

Directions:

1. Gather all the ingredients.
2. Pour a c. of grated cheese into a large microwave-friendly bowl.
3. Add 2 tbsp of white wine to it. Mix well.
4. Add a teaspoon of minced garlic to it. Also, sprinkle some salt and pepper according to your taste.
5. Microwave it for a few minutes.
6. Now, put a teaspoon of minced garlic, 1/3 cup of hazelnuts, and a teaspoon of cheese in a grinder. Grind well.
7. After this, add half a cup of basil leaves and two tablespoons of olive oil. Grind it again.
8. Take this fine paste out of the grinder and place it in the middle of the fondue prepared.
9. That is it. Pesto fondue is ready. Enjoy it while it's hot.

28. Crab Fondue

Prep time: 10 mins

Cooking time: 25 mins

Servings: 4

Ingredients:

- 2 tbsp wine
- 1 tsp lime juice
- 1 tsp minced garlic
- 1 tbsp cornstarch
- 1 c. cheese
- Salt as required
- Black pepper as required
- 1/2 c. de-shelled crabs
- 1 c. water
- 2 tbsp oil

Directions:

1. Heat 2 tbsp of wine in a pan.
2. Add a tsp of lime juice and 1 tsp of minced garlic to it. Mix well.
3. Now, take a bowl and add cheese to it. Put 1 tbsp of cornstarch in it.
4. Transfer the cheese and cornstarch mixture to the pan. Mix thoroughly.
5. Sprinkle some salt and pepper.
6. Make sure no lumps remain in the fondue.
7. Transfer it to the fondue pot and turn on the candle.
8. Put crabs in a pot over a medium flame. Add water to it.
9. Cook for some time to soften the crabs.
10. Drain the water.
11. Heat oil in a pan and add crabs to it. Cook for some time. Season with salt and pepper.
12. Transfer to a platter and enjoy with fondue.

29. Blackened Shrimp & Scallop Fondue

Prep time: 10 mins

Cooking time: 20 mins

Servings: 4

Ingredients:

- 1/2 c. butter
- 3 tbsp all-purpose flour
- 1 onion
- 1/2 c. grated cheese
- 1/2 c. wine
- Salt as required
- 1 c. heavy cream
- 5 oz shrimps
- 5 oz scallops
- 1 tbsp minced garlic
- 1 tsp paprika
- Black pepper as required
- 1 tsp onion powder
- 2 tbsp oil

Directions:

1. First, we will make the fondue. Start by melting butter in a pan.
2. Dice an onion and add it to the pan.
3. Add all-purpose flour and half a cup of grated parmesan cheese to the pan.
4. Pour some wine and sprinkle a little salt into the mix.
5. Lastly, add a cup of heavy cream.
6. Cook for a few more minutes and turn off the heat.
7. Transfer it to the fondue pot and proceed to prepare the scallops and shrimp
8. Heat oil in a saucepan. Add 1 tbsp of minced garlic.
9. Season the scallops and shrimp well with salt, black pepper, paprika, and onion powder.
10. Cook these in hot oil.
11. Turn off the heat and transfer to a plate. Serve with the fondue.

30. Spicy Crab Fondue

Prep time: 10 mins

Cooking time: 20 mins

Servings: 4

Ingredients

- 1/4 c. white dry wine
- 1/4 tsp garlic salt
- 1/2 tsp cayenne pepper
- 1/2 tsp Worcestershire sauce
- 1 c. crab meat, drained and flaked
- 1 package of cream cheese (8 oz. package)
- 5 oz sharp cheddar cheese
- 8 ½ oz French bread cut into cubes

Directions:

1. Combine the cheeses in a small pot until melted and smooth.
2. Add remaining ingredients. Stir well. If too thick, add additional wine.
3. Pour into a fondue pot with its own heat source to keep the mixture warm.
4. Serve with breadsticks or bread chunks of your choice.

31. Strawberry Fondue

Prep time: 10 mins

Cooking time: 20 mins

Servings: 4

Ingredients

- 1 c. vanilla yogurt
- Grated rind from one orange
- One can or tin of strawberries in juice

Directions:

1. As you grate the rind of the orange, be careful to extract only the orange rind, not the bitter white pith.

2. Drain the strawberries from the tin and discard the juice.

3. Put the strawberries into the fondue pot and mash with the back of a fork.

4. Add the yogurt and orange rind. Serve chilled with cubes of plain sponge cake or plain biscuits to dip.

32. Vegetarian Delight Fondue

Prep time: 10 mins

Cooking time: 30 mins

Servings: 4

Ingredients

- 1/4 c. milk
- 1/4 c. white wine
- 1 (8 oz) package shredded cheddar cheese
- 1 (8 oz) package shredded Monterey Jack cheese
- 1 (8 oz) package cream cheese, softened
- 1/4 c. chopped green onions
- ¼ c. frozen chopped spinach, thawed and drained
- 1 tsp ground dry mustard
- 1 tsp ground cayenne pepper
- 1 tsp garlic powder
- 1 tsp coarsely ground black pepper

Directions:

1. In a medium-sized saucepan over medium heat, mix together milk, white wine, Cheddar cheese, Monterey Jack cheese and cream cheese.

2. Cook for about 10 minutes and stir frequently until melted.

3. Stir in green onions, spinach, dry mustard, cayenne pepper, garlic powder and black pepper.

4. Continue cooking for 10 minutes until all ingredients are well blended,

5. Transfer the mixture to a double boiler or fondue pot to keep it warm. Perfect for roasted or raw veggie dippers.

33. Velvet Fondue

Prep time: 10 mins

Cooking time: 30 mins

Servings: 4

Ingredients

- 1 tbsp coffee liqueur
- 1/3 c. heavy whipping cream
- 4 ounces premium milk chocolate
- For fun, add 4-6 drops red food coloring

Directions:

1. Heat the cream in a small saucepan over low heat on your stovetop.

2. Once it's simmering, stir in chocolate and liqueur. Stir the mixture continuously until all of the chocolate melts.

3. Pour into a fondue pot with its own heat source to keep the mixture warm. Serve this red velvet treat with fruit.

34. Very Berry Fondue

Prep time: 10 mins

Cooking time: 30 mins

Servings: 4

Ingredients

- **1/2** c. caster sugar
- 1 lb. mixed summer fruits
- 6 tsp of corn flour
- Pinch of mixed spice

Directions:

1. Put the fruits into a saucepan with the sugar and 5 fl. oz of water, and cook gently until tender.
2. Crush fruits slightly with a potato masher and add the mixed spice.
3. In a small bowl, blend the cornflour smoothly with a little water.
4. Add this to the fruit in the pan and cook until thickened, stirring constantly. **Bring** to a boil.
5. Transfer to a fondue pot with its own heat source. Use dippers of your choice.

35. Very Vegan Potato Fondue

Prep time: 10 mins

Cooking time: 40 mins

Servings: 4

Ingredients

- 1 ½ tsp salt
- 1 c. dry white wine
- 1 pinch ground nutmeg
- 1 tbsp olive oil
- 10 small boiling potatoes, peeled (1 lb.)
- 2 large onions, peeled and chopped
- 2 tbsp cornstarch
- 2 tbsp nutritional yeast
- 3 cloves garlic, minced

Directions:

1. Cook potatoes in boiling, salted water 5 to 8 minutes, or until soft. Drain and set aside.

2. Heat oil in a medium saucepan over medium-low heat. Add onions, and cook for 15 to 20 mins, or until soft and translucent.

3. Add garlic, and cook for 1 to 2 additional minutes.

4. Meanwhile, dissolve cornstarch in 2 c. of cold water in a small bowl. Add cornstarch mixture to onion mixture, increase heat to medium, and simmer for 5 minutes, stirring occasionally.

5. Add yeast and salt, and simmer for 5 minutes more, stirring occasionally.

6. Remove from heat, and add potatoes and 1/2 cup of wine. Blend with a blender until smooth. Return to heat, and simmer gently for 5 minutes.

7. Add remaining 1/2 cup of wine, and cook 1 minute, stirring once or twice, or until fondue thickens.

8. Transfer to a fondue pot, sprinkle with nutmeg and serve with dippers. Try green apples!

36. White Cream Fondue

Prep time: 10 mins

Cooking time: 30 mins

Servings: 4

Ingredients

- 1 oz cherry brandy
- 12 oz white chocolate
- 8 oz double cream

Directions:

1. Combine the chocolate and cream in a bowl over a pan of hot water (or use a double boiler), and stir until the chocolate melts completely.

2. Remove the bowl from the heat and stir in the cherry brandy.

3. Put the mixture in a fondue pot to keep warm. Serve with pieces of fruit or firm cake.

37. White Wine Swirl Fondue

Prep time: 10 mins

Cooking time: 20 mins

Servings: 4

Ingredients

- 1/4 c. cherry brandy
- 1/2 clove garlic (optional)
- 1 lb. Swiss cheese, grated
- 2 c. dry white wine
- 2 dashes nutmeg
- 3 tbsp flour
- Black pepper

Directions:

1. Rub pot walls with butter.

2. Dredge cheese with flour. Heat wine on the stove to about 150°.

3. Add cheese by the handful, stirring until melted before each new addition.

4. When all cheese has melted and the mixture bubbles, add all seasonings (pepper, nutmeg and brandy.) Cook it slowly; simmering should take about 20 mins. Keep the heat on the low side to prevent burning. French bread, crisped in the oven and broken into hunks is the ideal dipper for this one.

38. Asparagus Glazed with white truffle fondue

Prep time: 10 mins

Cooking time: 20 mins

Servings: 4

Ingredients

- 2 tbsp Unsalted butter (1 ounce)
- 2 tbsp Minced shallots
- 1 lb. pencil-thin asparagus
- Salt and ground freshly pepper
- 1/4 c. White fondue truffle (from 3.5 oz jar)
- 1 tsp Minced tarragon

Directions:

1. Pre-heat up the oven and keep the position of the rack in the oven 8 inches away from the heat.
2. Take a large skillet and melt the butter, then add minced shallots; cook it over medium-high heat till now it softens for 1 minute.
3. Now add seasoning of pepper, salt and asparagus. Cook it over medium heat.
4. Stir until it gets crispy and lightly brown for 5 minutes.
5. Put the asparagus into a medium-sized gratin dish, now spread the fondue truffle over them.
6. Boil it until it bubbles and golden brown. Serve and sprinkle it with the tarragon.

39. Chocolate-Caramel Fondue

Prep time: 10 mins

Cooking time: 30 mins

Servings: 4

Ingredients:

- 1 can of 14 oz Condensed sweetened milk
- 1 jar of 12 oz Topping caramel ice cream
- 3 oz Chopped unsweetened chocolate
- Fresh assorted fruits or Pretzels

Directions:

1. Take a small saucepan, add and combine the milk, caramel, and chocolate topping.
2. Stir and cook it on low heat until it gets completely blended.
3. Transfer it to a warm fondue pot, and keep it warm.
4. Now serve it with fruits and pretzels and use it for dipping.

40. Bread Pot Fondue

Prep time: 10 mins

Cooking time: 20 mins

Servings: 4

Ingredients:

- 1 lb. Round loaf bread
- 1 pkg (8 oz) cheddar shredded cheese
- 2 pkg (3 oz) cream cheese
- 1 ½ c. Sour cream
- 1 c. diced cooked ham
- 1/2 c. green onion chopped
- 1 can (4 oz)Green peppers chile diced
- 1 tsp Worcestershire sauce
- 2 tbsp vegetable oil s
- 1 tbsp melted butter p

Directions:

1. Pre-heat the oven to 350F. From the top of the bread, cut it into a circle shape.
2. Remove the top of the bread loaf and keep it aside; reserve the rest of the bread for dipping.
3. Take a medium bowl; mix the cream cheese, cheddar cheese, ham, sour cream, chile green pepper, green onion, and Worcestershire sauce.
4. Put a spoonful of the mixture in the carved bread bowl..
5. Wrap foil paper around the bowl lightly and put it on a baking sheet.
6. Transfer it to the oven and bake it until the cheese becomes bubbly and melts for 1 hour.
7. Cut the reserved bread into slices.
8. Toss it with the melted butter and oil and keep it on the baking sheet.
9. Toast it in the oven for 10 - 15 minutes until it becomes golden brown. Now serve your amazing fondue with golden brown toast.

41. Roasted Butternut Squash Cheese Fondue

Prep time: 10 mins

Cooking time: 30 mins

Servings: 4

Ingredients:

- 2 c.. roasted butternut squash, pureed
- 1 c. dry white wine
- 2 c. gruyere cheese, grated
- 2 c. Swiss cheese, grated
- 2 tbsp. plain flour
- 1/4 tsp. salt and black pepper to taste

Directions:

1. Combine all the ingredients in a medium pot over medium heat and cook. Stir frequently for 4 minutes or until the cheeses melt.

2. Serve the fondue with your favorite dippers.

42. Mocha Fondue

Prep time: 10 mins

Cooking time: 20 mins

Servings: 4

Ingredients:

- 1 (14 oz.) canned sweetened condensed milk
- 1 (12 oz.) package semisweet chocolate morsels
- 1 c. miniature marshmallows
- 1/4 c. brewed strong coffee
- 1/2 c. Kahlua or other liqueur flavored coffee
- 1/3 c. pound cake cubes
- 1 c. angel food cake cubes
- 1/2 c. pear and apple slices

Directions:

1. In a medium-sized saucepan, combine the milk, chocolate morsels, marshmallows and coffee, then heat on low to medium heat.
2. Cook and continuously stir until the chocolate melts and the mixture becomes smooth.
3. Now, stir it in Kahlua; Pour the mix into a fondue pot.
4. Put it on the fondue burner.
5. Serve it with the fruit slices and cake cubes as a dipper.
6. Enjoy it to the fullest.

43. Butterscotch Fondue

Prep time: 10 mins

Cooking time: 25 mins

Servings: 4

Ingredients:

- 2 tbsp. golden syrup
- 2 tbsp. sugar
- 3 tsp. butter
- 1/2 c. heavy cream
- 1 tsp. vanilla
- 1 apple, sliced
- 1 pear, sliced

Directions:

1. Add the golden syrup, sugar and butter to a pan. Boil for 5 mins
2.
3. Add the heavy cream and vanilla.
4. Stir well and let it thicken.
5. Transfer to a bowl.
6. Serve with the apple and pear slices.

44. Luscious Caramel Fondue

Prep time: 10 mins

Cooking time: 30 mins

Servings: 4

Ingredients:

- 1 split vanilla bean with the seeds scraped out
- 1/4 c. water
- 1 c. heavy cream
- 2 c. granulated sugar
- 1 c. your favorite dipping ingredients

Directions:

1. Combine the water with the sugar in a medium-sized saucepan. Cook on medium-low heat. Stir until the sugar dissolves.

2. Cover the pan. Bring to a boil. Leave covered for a minute.

3. Raise the heat to medium-high. Do not stir. Swirl the pan while cooking until the color of the mixture is darkened amber. Add the cream CAREFULLY as it will splatter.

4. Add the vanilla beans and whisk and combine. Transfer the mixture to your fondue pot. Set over a warming candle. Serve promptly with the assorted dipping ingredients.

45. Fondue S'mores

Prep time: 10 mins

Cooking time: 25 Minutes

Servings: 4

Ingredients:

- 1/4 c. graham crackers, crumbled
- 2 c. miniature marshmallows
- 1/3 c. heavy cream
- 1½ c. marshmallow cream
- 24 oz. milk chocolate
- 1 c. marshmallows, strawberries, graham crackers, etc. for dipping

Directions:

1. Mix the heavy cream, chocolate and marshmallow cream in a medium-sized saucepan on low heat. Allow the ingredients to melt and stir until the mixture is creamy.

2. Heat the broiler. Place the miniature marshmallows on a baking sheet. Broil until they are lightly browned.

3. Pour the mixture from the saucepan into a fondue pot. Top with the crumbled graham crackers and broiled marshmallows. Serve with marshmallows, whole graham crackers, and strawberries.

46. Spiced Apple Fondue

Prep time: 10 mins

Cooking time: 20 mins

Servings: 4

Ingredients

- 1/4 c. half and half
- 1 ¾ c. semisweet chocolate chips
- 1/2 tsp ground cinnamon
- 2 tbsp apple schnapps
- 3 medium Spartan apples, cored and cut into wedges

Directions:

1. Combine half and half and chocolate in a medium-sized metal bowl. Place the bowl over a saucepan half filled with simmering water. Melt chips over low to medium-low heat, stirring continuously and making sure the mixture doesn't boil.

2. When the chocolate is melted, transfer the mixture to the fondue pot and set over the heat source. Stir in cinnamon and apple schnapps. Keep the fondue warm over low heat. Serve with apple wedges for dipping.

47. Yin-Yang Fondue

Prep time: 10 mins

Cooking time: 30 mins

Servings: 4

Ingredients

8 oz white chocolate, broken into pieces

8 oz semisweet chocolate, broken into pieces

1/2 c. evaporated milk

1/2 tsp ground cinnamon

1/4 c. kirsch

6 c. mixed apple and cantaloupe slices

Directions:

1. In a medium-sized metal bowl, combine white chocolate, semisweet chocolate, and evaporated milk.

2. Place the bowl on top of a saucepan half filled with simmering water. Melt the mixture on low to medium-low heat, making sure that it doesn't boil.

3. When the chocolate has melted, stir in cinnamon and kirsch.

4. Transfer the fondue mixture to the fondue pot and set it over the heat source. Keep the fondue warm on low heat. Serve with apple and cantaloupe slices for dipping.

48. Tiramisu with Cream Fondue

Prep time: 10 mins

Cooking time: 25 mins

Servings: 4

Ingredients

- 1 pound mascarpone cheese
- 1/4 c. light cream
- 1/4 c. confectioners' sugar
- 1/4 c. strong, fresh-brewed espresso coffee, divided
- 1 tbsp plus 1 tsp powdered hot chocolate
- 2 tsp cornstarch
- 2 tbsp rum
- 4 large egg yolks
- 2 tsp ground cinnamon
- 24 ladyfingers

Directions:

1. In a medium-sized metal bowl, combine mascarpone, light cream, confectioners' sugar, and 4 tsp espresso. Place the bowl on top of a saucepan half filled with simmering water. Melt mixture over low to medium-low heat, stirring frequently and making sure that it doesn't boil.

2. When mascarpone has melted and has a texture close to pudding, stir in hot chocolate.

3. In a small bowl, dissolve cornstarch in rum. Stir the mixture into the fondue.

4. Whisk in egg yolks to thicken.

5. Transfer the fondue mixture to the fondue pot and set it over the heat source. Keep warm over low heat. Just before serving, sprinkle it with cinnamon.

6. Brush ladyfingers with remaining espresso and serve with the fondue for dipping.

49. Doughnut Fondue

Prep time: 10 mins

Cooking time: 20 mins

Servings: 4

Ingredients

- 8 ounces semisweet chocolate, broken into pieces
- 1 c. cinnamon baking chips
- 6 tbsp sour cream
- 6 tbsp evaporated milk
- 1/4 c. half and half
- 2 tbsp butter
- 1/4 tsp ground allspice
- Plain doughnuts

Directions:

1. In a medium metal bowl, combine chocolate, baking chips, sour cream, evaporated milk, and half and half and place the bowl on top of a saucepan half filled with simmering water. Melt the mixture over low to medium-low heat, making sure that it doesn't boil.

2. Add butter and allow to melt. Stir in allspice.

3. Transfer the fondue mixture to a fondue pot and set over the heat source. Keep the fondue warm over low heat.

4. Serve with doughnuts for dipping. Doughnuts can be eaten whole or cut into pieces and speared with a dipping fork.

50. Spiced Apple Fondue

Prep time: 10 mins

Cooking time: 25 Minutes

Servings: 4

Ingredients

- **1/4** c. half and half
- 1 ¾ c. semisweet chocolate chips
- 1/2 tsp ground cinnamon
- 2 tbsp apple schnapps
- 3 medium Spartan apples, cored and cut into wedges

Directions:

1. In a medium metal bowl, combine half and half and chocolate and place the bowl over a saucepan half filled with simmering water. Melt chips over low to medium-low heat, stirring continuously and making sure the mixture doesn't boil.

2. When the chocolate is melted, transfer the mixture to the fondue pot and set over the heat source. Stir in cinnamon and apple schnapps. Keep the fondue warm over low heat. Serve with apple wedges for dipping.

51. Sweet-and-Sour Tropical Fondue

Prep time: 10 mins

Cooking time: 20 mins

Servings: 4

Ingredients

- **3/4** c. sour cream
- 2 tbsp butter
- 2 c. chocolate macaroons
- 2 tbsp Kahlúa
- 4 medium bananas, peeled and sliced
- 2 c. tropical dried fruit mix

Directions:

1. In a medium metal bowl, combine sour cream, butter, and chocolate macaroons and place the bowl over a saucepan half filled with simmering water. Heat mixture over medium-low heat, stirring constantly. Do not let the mixture boil.

2. When the chocolate is melted, stir in Kahlúa. Transfer the mixture to the fondue pot and set over the heat source. Keep the fondue warm over low heat.

3. Serve with bananas and dried fruit for dipping

52. Comte Fondue

Prep time: 10 mins

Cooking time: 20 mins

Servings: 8 – 10

Ingredients:

- 900g mature Comte cheese, grated
- 2 cloves garlic, peeled
- 4 tsp Kirsch
- Freshly ground pepper to taste
- ½ tsp ground cumin or to taste (optional)
- 2 ½ c. dry white wine
- 2 tbsp cornstarch
- ¼ c. sliced wild mushrooms like cepes
- 10 – 12 Asperula Odorata or tarragon leaves or rosemary leaves (optional)
- Salt to taste (optional)

Directions:

1. Add kirsch and cornstarch into a bowl and stir.
2. Add cheese, garlic and wine into the fondue pot or heavy-bottomed saucepan.
3. Place the pot over low heat until the cheese melts. Stir frequently.
4. Add mushrooms and herbs and stir.
5. Add most of the cornstarch mixture and stir constantly until it thickens. If you find that the fondue is not thickening, add the remaining cornstarch and stir until thick.
6. Add pepper, salt and cumin and mix well. Turn off the heat.
7. Transfer into a bowl and serve.

53. Fondue Savoyarde

Prep time: 10 mins

Cooking time: 10 mins

Servings: 12

Ingredients:

- 400g comte gouda cheese, grated
- 400g Reblochon cheese, grated
- 400g Beaufort cheese, grated
- 1 large garlic clove
- 2 tbsp cornstarch
- 5 c. dry white wine
- 6 tbsp sour cherry brandy or Kirsch
- 1/4 tsp freshly grated nutmeg
- 1/8 tsp paprika
- Salt to taste (optional)

Directions:

1. Cut garlic into 2 halves and rub the inside of the fondue pot with it. Throw away the garlic cloves.
2. Add all the cheese into a bowl. Toss well.
3. Add wine and cornstarch into the prepared fondue pot and whisk thoroughly.
4. Place the pot over medium-low heat. When it begins to simmer, add the cheese mixture into the pot, a handful at a time and mix well each time.
5. When all has been added, stir until smooth. Add nutmeg, paprika, pepper and salt and stir. Let it simmer until the desired thickness is achieved. Turn off the heat.
6. Transfer into a bowl and serve.

54. Camembert Fondue

Prep time: 10 mins

Cooking time: 30 mins

Servings: 8

Ingredients:

- 2 boxes (255g each) boxed Camembert cheese
- 2 tbsp olive oil
- 2 sprigs rosemary
- 4 sprigs thyme
- Salt to taste
- Freshly ground pepper to taste
- 4 tbsp honey

Directions:

1. Remove the cheese from the refrigerator and place on your countertop for 30 mins.
2. Take out the cheese from the boxes and remove the wrapping. Cut off the top rind of the cheese.
3. Place the cheese back into the boxes, with the cut side facing up. Place thyme and rosemary over the cheese. Dribble honey and oil over the cheese.
4. Line a baking sheet with baking paper. Place the boxes on the baking sheet.
5. Bake in a preheated oven at 350° F for about 20 – 25 minutes or until the cheese melts.
6. Remove from the oven and cool for a few minutes. Serve

CHAPTER 4: FAQ

What Are The Different Types of Fondue?

From Savory to Sweet Fondue

There are no hard and fast rules when it comes to making fondue. Simply select the ingredients and combine them. Once they're smooth and saucy, transfer them to your fondue pot, place them in the center of the dining table with your dipping ingredients, and you've got yourself a fondue party.

You do not actually need to be a pro in cooking to arrange a fondue party either. As long as you can stand in front of a stove and stir something in a pot, you got this! The sole query is whether you're cooking a sweet or savory fondue. Your choice!

Cheese

At their most basic forms, fondues are made of cheese or a combination of different cheeses, mixed and matched with preferred flavoring. This is the Swiss traditional way of doing it. You can also take inspiration from French cooks, who make delectable oil-based fondues which they bathe their meats into. You can decide to opt for the Chinese way in which a broth is used instead of a cheesy sauce.

The American Way: Tasty and Chocolatey

The sweet, rich, and creamy fondues, on the other hand, are led by America's well-received version of the Chocolate Fondue. Every party or event has a dessert buffet, and in the middle of it all, standing tall and swirling a sweet concoction, is a fondue pot. As with the savory fondues, variations arose from the classic.

A few chocolate versions and other syrupy sweet mixes are worth noting so you can impress as a certified fondue master the next time.

To Wine Or Not To Wine?

Fondue is traditionally made with a wine or beer emulsion and cheese. The tartaric acid in wine aids in the emulsification of the cheese into the liquid, resulting in a more luxurious cheese fondue. This combination has a delicious flavor, but it is not for everyone. If you don't want to use alcohol in your fondue, you can easily replace it with the same amount of good-quality vegetable or chicken broth. If you don't use wine in your fondue, thicken the liquid with cornstarch before adding the cheese to ensure proper emulsification. The broth will add flavor, so choose one that complements the other fondue components.

Why Does Good Cheese Matters?

When making fondue, it is reasonable to select the best-quality cheese for your budget. Traditional whole milk cheese has layers of flavor that translate into a superior pot of cheese fondue. AOC (Appellation d'Origine Contrôlée) or DOP (Denominazione di Origine Protetta) certification is commonly found on European cheeses. Both acronyms translate to "Protected Designation of Origin," which means that the cheeses come from a specific geographical region or area and are made according to a protected recipe that accounts for animal care and feed, milk quality, and specific parameters in the production and aging of the cheese. These distinctions ensure that you are purchasing a genuine piece of cheese. Locally made cheeses are also a good option, especially if they come from a reputable producer who uses natural cheesemaking methods. Look for cheeses made in the same style as the one listed in your recipe, and don't be afraid to try something new! Because cheese fondue requires only a few simple ingredients, take the time to select cheese varieties that will yield the best results.

What should you stock in your Fondue Pantry?

It is simple to serve fondue on a whim with a well-stocked pantry. Since most of the recipes in this book come together in less than 30 minutes, fondue is a viable meal option for any night of the week. Use this list to keep a selection of fondue pantry essentials on hand.

- Brandy. This spirit is used to add a sharp and heady bite to both sweet and savory fondue.

- Broth, chicken and beef. Since there are very few ingredients used in fondue, the flavor and quality of your broth make a difference. Choose higher-quality, ready-made broth over bouillon cubes, or use our recipe for Classic Beef Broth and Chicken Broth.

- Oil for cooking. Peanut, sunflower seed, and safflower seed oil are flavorless and have high smoke points, making them ideal for frying.

- Cornstarch. This is the main thickening agent in this cookbook. It produces a smooth, emulsified cheese fondue.

- Mustard from Dijon. This is an excellent mustard for emulsifying sauces and adding a spicy bite and well-rounded flavor to almost any cheese dish or sauce.

- Dry White wine. Although most cheese fondue recipes can be made without wine, it is the preferred liquid because it adds flavor and aids in the emulsification of the cheese.

- Vacuum-packed milk. In a pinch, evaporated milk can be used in place of heavy cream. Your cheese fondue, dessert custard, or caramel sauce will have a creamy texture as a result.

- Garlic. This herb enhances the flavor of the broth, cheese fondue, and sauces.

- Mayonnaise. Many of the sauce recipes in this book use mayonnaise as a base. Make your own right here.

- Onions. Caramelize them for French Onion Broth and Fondue, or add them to any broth for flavoring.

- Peanut butter. Peanut dipping sauce is quick to make and adds flavor and intrigue to your fondue experience. It also goes well with chocolate.

- Semisweet Chocolate. The best chocolate you can afford should be chosen, and the flavors should be highlighted.

- Sugar. It is the most important ingredient for making homemade caramel and adding sweetness to your dessert fondue.

How do you Set the Fondue Table?

Fondue can be a relaxing way to enjoy a social meal, but it can quickly become crowded and messy if not properly planned. You can decide what you need to do in order to maximize your seating and service arrangements by using the following checklist.

- Basket for dipping. This is a small metal basket that is ideal for cooking vegetables and noodles in hot broth fondue.

- A lighter and extra fuel if you're using a fondue pot with an open-flame heat source, keep extra fuel and a lighter on hand. If you run out of fuel, your fondue will quickly become cold.

- Fondue pan. This pot, also known as a caquelon, is the showpiece and will keep your fondue warm until the pot is empty.

- Forks with long handles. Each guest should have their own fondue fork with a long handle for dipping into the fondue pot. Choose a color-coded set so guests can keep track of their forks in the pot.

- Paper Towels. Place a few layers of paper towels on a plate near the pot when serving hot oil fondue to drain fried foods as they cool.

- Plates. At their seat, each guest should be given their own plate for assembling a plate of dippers and resting their fondue forks between dips. If you intend to make fondue a regular event, invest in raclette plates with divided sections.

- Ramekins. Provide a choice of two or three sauces in ramekins with a small spoon.

- Glasses for shots. To aid digestion, heavy cheese and hot oil fondue are traditionally served with an intermission shot of Kirschwasser or another spirit of your choice.

- Napkins and tablecloth. Fondue can be a messy affair, so use a tablecloth to protect your table from spills and splatters. Allow your guests to bring their own napkins, and keep a few extra on hand just in case.

- Thermometer. If you're serving hot oil or broth-style fondue and cooking meats and seafood, it's a good idea to keep a thermometer nearby to ensure proper cooking temperatures.

- Tongs. If you need to reach a lost dipper at the bottom of the pot, use tongs instead of your fondue fork.

- Wine, beer, or cocktail glasses. Wine is the traditional beverage served with fondue, but your guests may enjoy any beverage of their choosing. It is best to actually avoid drinking water when serving cheese fondue, as water can make the cheese feel very heavy in your stomach.

CONCLUSION

Thank you for reading this cookbook. Fondues are extremely versatile. In fact, they can include anything from savory to sweet. However, regardless of their flavor profile, fondues are some of the best party superstars you should learn to make. The ability to prepare the most appropriate dipping ingredients, whether fruits, vegetables, bread, meats, or a combination of all, is the key to hosting a successful fondue party. Mix and match dipping ingredients that are in season and easy to obtain, and, of course, make sure they taste delicious with your dipping sauce.

Fondue was originally created as a winter dish to be eaten during times of scarcity, but it has since grown to be an international favorite. This cookbook contains a collection of quick and easy recipes suitable for any weather and occasion. These recipes are ideal for entertaining guests or simply cooking with family and friends this winter. They will keep you warm and satisfied. It's simple to make them at home!

Make a list of your favorite recipes and save them for special occasions. Also, make your children eat all of these recipes; they will fall in love. Experiment with some recipes by incorporating your favorite ingredients. We guarantee that you will enjoy every course.

You can begin experimenting once you understand the various flavor combinations that work well together. All of the recipes in this book are not only simple to understand, but also simple to prepare.

When making a fondue, make sure to use high-quality cheese. It's a little pricey, but it definitely improves the flavor of the fondue. Grate the cheese rather than chop it to get a smooth fondue that melts quickly. If you don't want lumpy fondue, thoroughly coat the cheese with cornstarch. Using wine to make fondue is not only fashionable, but it also results in a smooth and silky texture. Additionally, be sure to use premium wines that are acidic and dry. The acid in the wine avoids clumping and prevents the sauce from breaking.

Before throwing a party, make sure you have enough fondue skewers and forks for all of your guests. You can make the fondue ahead of time, refrigerate it, and then gently reheat it in a double boiler. Cooking delicious food is actually quite simple.

All that remains is for you to purchase all of the necessary ingredients and get started! So, what are you holding out for? Good luck.

ALPHABETICAL INDEX

Made in United States
Troutdale, OR
01/08/2024